THE
NFL
EXPERIENCE

TWELVE MONTHS WITH AMERICA'S FAVORITE GAME

Text by
PHIL BARBER

DK Publishing

IN ASSOCIATION WITH THE NATIONAL FOOTBALL LEAGUE

NFL Publishing Group

The NFL Experience
TWELVE MONTHS WITH AMERICA'S FAVORITE GAME

NFL PUBLISHING
Editor-in-Chief John Wiebusch
General Manager Bill Barron
The NFL Experience **Editor** Tom Barnidge
Managing Editor John Fawaz
Executive Art Director Brad Jansen
The NFL Experience **Art Director** Bill Madrid
Director-Photo Services Paul Spinelli
Photo Editor Kevin Terrell
Manager-Photo Services Tina Resnick
Director-Manufacturing Dick Falk
Director-Print Services Tina Dahl
Manager-Computer Graphics Sandy Gordon
Publishing Director Bob O'Keefe
Publishing Manager Lori Quenneville

DK PUBLISHING
Publisher Sean Moore
Editorial Director Chuck Wills
Art Director Dirk Kaufman

First American Edition, 2001
10 9 8 7 6 5 4 3 2 1
Published in the United States by
DK Publishing, Inc.
95 Madison Avenue
New York, New York 10016

A catalog record for this book is available from the Library of
Congress.

Produced by National Football League
Publishing Division
6701 Center Drive West, Suite 1111
Los Angeles, California 90045

Printed in Spain by Artes Gráficas Toledo S.A.U.
D.L. TO: 726-2001

DK Publishing books are available at special discounts for bulk
purchases for sales promotions or premiums. Special editions,
including personalized covers, excerpts of existing guides, and
corporate imprints can be created in large quantities for specific
needs. For more information, contact Special Markets Dept./DK
Publishing, Inc./95 Madison Avenue/New York, New York 10016/
FAX: 800-600-9098

CONTENTS

THE STUFF OF GLADIATORS

BY PHIL BARBER

You probably have heard the comment, from a repairman or a coworker or your neighbor who once was a high-school quarterback. They see NFL players on TV, made glorious in super-slow-mo. They read about a wide receiver who received an $8 million signing bonus. And they shake their heads and say, "Man, I could have played this game."

If only it were that easy.

Pro football players are admired primarily for their physical attributes. They all look like Marvel Comics characters nowadays, with biceps sharp enough to etch glass. A typical offensive lineman weighs 300 pounds and moves like a mama grizzly protecting her cubs. Even the quarterbacks are weighing in at more more than 250.

But you could walk into a health club in just about any city in America and find a dozen men who look just like them. We have no shortage of modern-day Atlases.

The thing is, pure physical ability never has been the sole requirement for playing in the NFL. It's only the first one. You do have to be somewhat larger than life, or faster than light, to play in the NFL. But pro football players are special for more reasons than their athletic talent.

This is not necessarily a popular view. The knee-jerk characterization of the NFL player is of an overpaid, undersupervised brute. He's the boy who never grew up, and now he's driving a Range Rover with all the options.

Are NFL players really overpaid? No more than any other professional entertainer. And like motion picture actors and pop stars, they benefit from our insatiable desire to be entertained. Can you blame any of them for accepting the money? If you were 27 years old, with a family to support and a career that could end with any awkward foot plant or helmet-to-helmet hit, you'd do the same.

So begrudge them their riches. But don't minimize the price they paid to arrive at their station. Pro football players work harder than most of us, and their coaches work harder than that.

Watching an NFL game and saying "I can do that" is like sitting on your front porch with a cup of coffee, watching runners in the the Boston Marathon race by, and saying, "I could finish this race."

NFL players must absorb playbooks the size of phone directories, then sit through endless classroom lectures and film work. Every time they switch teams—or welcome a new coach—they have to learn new terminology, if not an entire language. And while refining their assignments and techniques, they must be able to analyze and recognize their opponents' tendencies on a weekly basis.

On the field, if everything goes right, the hours of study are translated into reflex and action—against opponents just as large and talented as they are.

We say 'We're going to run this defense because we're anticipating that on this down, at this distance, in this part of the field, this is what they like to do,'" former linebacker Matt Millen explains. "So we're going to anticipate this particular set and this particular play. But we don't know. This is our best guess, and we're gonna react to it. Now, within the context of that, when they get to the line of scrimmage, to be a good defensive player, you have to think. And to be a great one, you have to start to eliminate options.

"The offense comes to the line of scrimmage. Now I see personnel. Do they have three wide receivers? That tells me something. If they have two tight ends and two backs, that tells me something. Based upon personnel, you start eliminating certain plays. By the time [the quarterback] has put his hands under the center's rear end, a bright defender will have eliminated three-quarters or more of what the offense can run."

It isn't just the mental preparation or the grueling fitness regimen that separates NFL players from the pack. There is a psychological edge to this profession that most of us will never fully appreciate.

Imagine performing your job—installing computer systems, negotiating contracts, writing a script—while 60,000 people scream at you to do it right, or root for you to get it wrong. The wonder is that any quarterback ever completes a pass. Mess up a few times, and you won't be able to tune in to AM radio without hearing someone you've never met telling the whole world how badly you performed. Warren Moon, one of the finest quarterbacks of his era, fell prey to a wild comeback by the Buffalo Bills in a 1992 playoff game, then held his children out of school the

Only the rarest of individuals have what it takes to carve out a career in the NFL.

next day. He couldn't bear to subject them to the inevitable taunts he knew they would hear.

And then there is the maelstrom of the game itself. The metaphors—tackling cars on the interstate, hiking in a forest where the trees come to life and attack—never quite do justice to the chaos. Pro football is fierce, complicated, exhausting, and undeniably painful. Injuries that would put most of us in bed, propped up with pillows, get NFL players listed as "probable" for the next weekend.

Quarterbacks are supposed to be the least physical of football players. But Boomer Esiason played the position for 14 NFL seasons, and this is how he describes it: "The guy [is] in the pocket, and the pass protection in front of him is parting like the Red Sea, and you know one of those defensive linemen is looping around to come up the middle, and [the quarterback] knows he's gotta hold the ball for a fraction longer, and when he throws it, he's gonna get hit underneath the chin. What the coaches are looking for is that guy who's going to stand in there and throw the ball accurately in the face of fire. To do it you have to have courage and stamina and stability."

Multiply that scene by 22 players and you have described NFL football.

Not to overstate. Football still is a game as much as a business. It doesn't affect the ocean tides or decide presidential elections. But if you can watch two NFL teams grapple on a Sunday afternoon and get lost in their efforts, if you can comprehend the hours of drills and practices that preceded that game, if you can appreciate the collective courage and stamina that is required to go all out for three hours on a Sunday afternoon, you will enjoy what follows on these pages.

THE GREATEST SHOW ON TURF

The Super Bowl is notoriously hard on municipal wastewater systems—all that simultaneous flushing at halftime. On the positive side, the National Football League's annual championship game helps keep crime off the streets.

During the Chiefs' victory over the Vikings in Super Bowl IV, the Kansas City Police Department reported exactly one burglary. Officers waited until halftime to interrogate the suspect, but it was the suspect who asked the first question: "What's the score?"

The Super Bowl has featured some of the greatest athletes ever to hoist a ball, from Bart Starr to Lynn Swann to Kurt Warner. It has offered us countless big plays and a few adrenalin-depleting conclusions. But the surrounding atmosphere—the hospitality tents, the Blue Angels, Japanese reporters, and American flags the size of Rhode Island—has become an equal measure of the Super Bowl experience.

It wasn't always so.

"I can remember the morning of the first one," said John Steadman, long-time columnist for the *Baltimore Sun*. "I was walking back from church with [some NFL executives] and we agreed that the Super Bowl didn't have much of a future."

It wasn't even the Super Bowl yet. Two years away from Roman numerals, it was merely the 1967 AFL-NFL World Championship Game, a novelty invented to give credibility to the impending merger. The inaugural game was played at the Los Angeles Coliseum, which was only two-thirds filled on a smoggy afternoon. Some people thought the NFL Pro Bowl, scheduled one week later at the same venue, was the more intriguing event. Only 338 print journalists showed up for the first Super Bowl, fitting neatly into the Coliseum press box. If reporters wished to interview someone, be it Green Bay full-

The entertainment begins long before kickoff at Super Bowl XXXV.

back Jim Taylor or NFL Commissioner Pete Rozelle, they simply knocked on the appropriate hotel room door and moved the luggage off the bed.

That was the calm before SuperBowl.com. That was before KISS and Queen Latifah, before the digital first-down stripes and four-hour pregame shows. That was when the Super Bowl was a mere football game. Now it comes loaded with a few accessories—such as the Super Bowl Golf Classic, The NFL Experience theme park, Super Bowl Youth Football Clinics, the *Lineman Challenge,* Taste of the NFL, NFL Passion for Fashion Show, Air-It-Out Flag Football, AFTI Global Junior Championship, *MTV Rock 'n' Jock Bowl,* NFL Youth Education Town, Super Bowl Card Show, and entertainment spectacles before kickoff and at halftime. Yes, they still find time to play the game.

In 1968, Packers coach Vince Lombardi went nuts when a TV crew sought shots of four players on a trampoline with Miss Florida Sunshine. If he were involved now, Lombardi might lay waste to the entire Super Bowl village.

So how did this happen? When did the Super Bowl take on the importance of an approaching meteorite?

Was it when the Jets and Chiefs scored upsets in III and IV, legitimizing the AFL-NFL merger? Was it Super Bowl X, when the blue-collar Pittsburgh Steelers and the streamlined Dallas Cowboys duked it out to launch the U.S. bicentennial? Was it two years later, when the NFL brought in legendary Disney producer Bob Jani to spice up the halftime show? Or was it during Super Bowl XVIII, when Apple Computer's ominous "1984" commercial made sponsors realize just how valuable 30 seconds of Super Bowl programming could be?

Ray Charles: one in a long line of Super Bowl stars

It's hard to say. Like the drift of American popular culture toward the grandiose and the dazzling, the Super Bowl's growth has come gradually.

Whatever the reasons, this game long ago exceeded its original dimensions. The first Super Bowl was broadcast to two countries, the United States and Canada. Super Bowl XXXV went out to 175 nations (at least), and the best-positioned 30-second commercial slots went for $2.3 million each. One poll found that approximately seven percent of all Super Bowl viewers—some 10 million people—tune in solely to watch the commercials.

There isn't much that brings America together these days. We speak in many tongues, celebrate a variety of religious holidays. Many of us don't even vote on Election Day. But just about everyone you can think of watches the Super Bowl. Financiers on Long Island, farmers in Ohio, propane salesmen in Texas, rappers in Los Angeles—all of them are glued to the same picture, share the same level of comfort, suggest the same plays.

So let the show begin. Let the corporate sponsors eat their weight in shrimp cocktail. Let Whitney Houston sing the National Anthem against a backdrop of war. Let John Madden telestrate the sweat stains of the Cowboys' offensive linemen. Let Michael Jackson dance behind the fog machines. Let Diana Ross be lifted from midfield by a helicopter. Let the airplanes circle stadiums like gnats with banners. Let the Budweiser amphibians croak one-liners. Let Mike Jones meet Kevin Dyson at the 1-yard line, an entire season hanging in the balance.

Each of us watches the Super Bowl for a different reason. The point is, we all watch.

Even halftime is a memorable spectacle at the biggest game of the year.

Whitney Houston ignites patriotic fervor with a stirring rendition of the National Anthem at Super Bowl XXV.

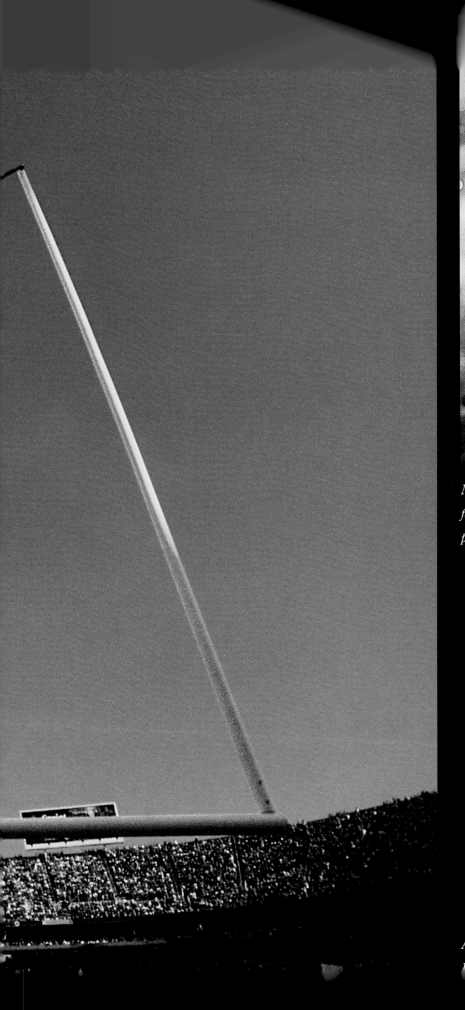

Michael Jackson brings Super Bowl fans to their feet with a dazzling combination of pop music and pyrotechnics at Super Bowl XXVII.

A military flyover at Qualcomm Stadium in San Diego sets the stage for Super Bowl XXXII.

Fireworks punctuate the halftime show at Super Bowl XXXI.

Reporters and photographers engulf the participants on Media Day—five days before the game.

A star player such as Brett Favre finds a lot of microphones stuck in his face during the week before the Super Bowl.

Warner QB 15:00 Rams ST. LO

RAMP F:
Media Access to

Press Box
Auxiliary Press
NFL International Booths
Media Phone Pass-out
ELEVATOR 3:
Disabled Media

*One of the biggest challenges of every Super Bowl is
directing all involved to their proper destinations.*

Kurt Warner trots into the national spotlight as introductions are made prior to Super Bowl XXXIV.

Pro football is the only focus on Super Bowl Sunday.

*No location is too obscure or camera angle too
remote for the network that broadcasts the game.*

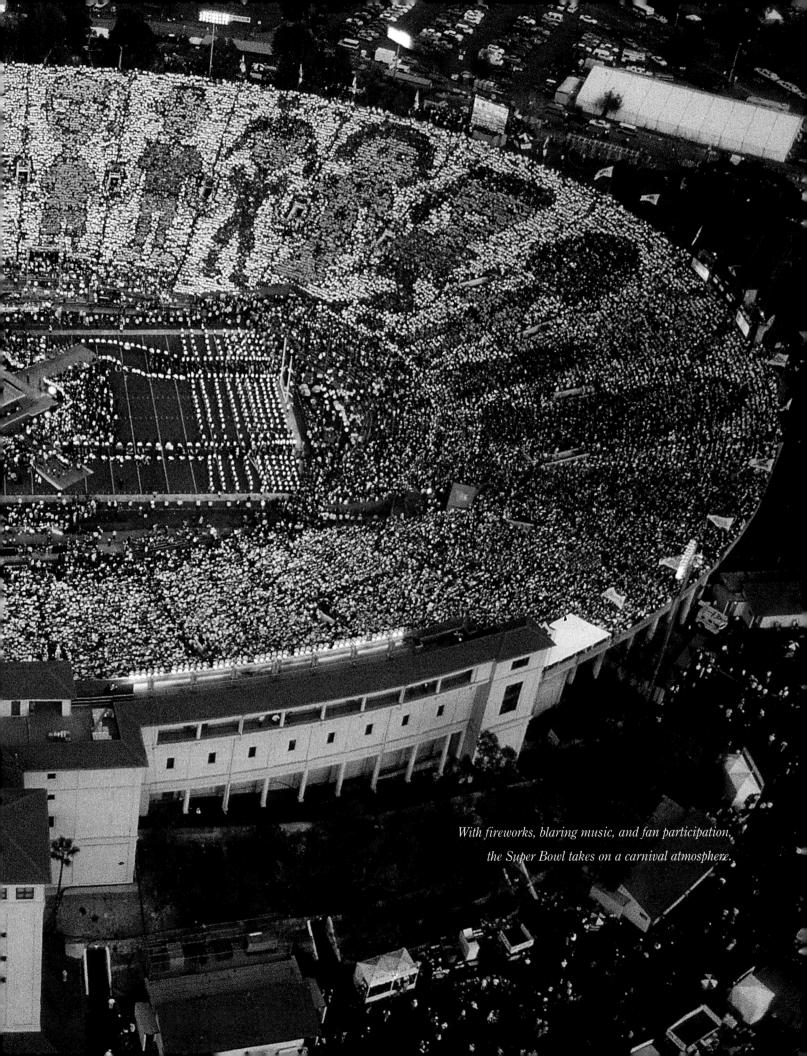

*With fireworks, blaring music, and fan participation,
the Super Bowl takes on a carnival atmosphere.*

Few rituals match the joy of a Super Bowl victory celebration.

OFFSEASON? WHAT OFFSEASON?

When Chuck Bednarik played center and linebacker for the Philadelphia Eagles, he was known as Concrete Charley. The nickname required no explanation for anyone who witnessed Bednarik's rock-hard demeanor and concussive hits on the field. But it had even more practical origins: The man sold concrete in the offseason.

Bednarik needed temporary work to make ends meet between January and July, and he wasn't alone among players of the pre-Super Bowl era. Cal Hubbard umpired baseball games in the spring. Ernie Stautner developed his forearms by hauling ice. The immortal Red Grange—one of the most celebrated stars of his day, the man who wore full-length raccoon coats and "saved pro football" in 1925—sold insurance door-to-door after going broke during the stock market crash of 1929.

Today's football players, compensated handsomely by their NFL teams, face no such economic imperatives. That doesn't mean they relax between seasons.

Remember the offseason? Younger NFL players don't. The league they know is a 12-month endeavor, in which men who show up to training camp out of shape might soon find themselves out of work.

Hauling ice sounds downright pleasant compared to the self-applied torture of some modern NFL players. Vikings defensive tackle John Randle has been known to rope a log to his waist and pull it up and down hills. Buccaneers fullback Mike Alstott prefers dragging a midsize automobile through a parking lot. Junior Seau, a perennial Pro Bowl linebacker, spends much of his offseason in the gym.

They are among the most extreme examples, but they are emblematic of an industry that demands ever greater commitments of time and sweat.

Strong-armed quarterback Kurt Warner works on his most important assets.

The money that has infused the game—the same money that makes second jobs unnecessary—has ratcheted competition levels to phobic heights. Pro football really is a profession now, and it is treated accordingly by its employees. Players can't afford to lose their physical or mental edge because the gap that separates first and second string has become razor thin.

There was a time when training camp was for getting in shape. Now players are expected to be in shape when they arrive.

So the sounds of boot camp have moved up to the springtime, to May and June minicamps and the voluntary workouts that precede them. The suggestion of "voluntary workouts" might have caused old Raiders such as Ken Stabler and Ted Hendricks to spill their cocktails as they convulsed with laughter. Now, teams routinely pull in the majority of locally residing players for optional weight training and track work in winter and spring. NFL bodies are expected to stay sharp all year long.

It has become even more intense for management. NFL coaches generally allow themselves two or three blissful weeks to unwind after the rigors of the season. Then they're back to work, the successes of the previous campaign quickly sublimated as they turn their attention to holes in the depth chart.

February brings the NFL Scouting Combine in Indianapolis, where scouts and personnel directors from every team gather to time, measure, weigh, quiz, and otherwise scrutinize the finest talent emerging from the college landscape. For the collegians, this is their first big chance to angle for a higher draft position. Some will strategically skip the combine altogether.

Chargers linebacker Junior Seau has been selected to 10 Pro Bowls in no small part because of his offseason work ethic.

Most will schedule individual workouts for a limited number of teams, knowing that every tenth of a second they shave off their 40-yard dash time can translate to hundreds of thousands of dollars. Now that's an adrenaline boost.

The draft comes in April, and the annual event has become an epic operation. NFL teams call their draft headquarters "war rooms," and NO SMOKING signs are ignored.

Grown men spend days trapped inside windowless rooms, sipping coffee, eating cold pizza, and working the phones more frantically than a pledge-drive volunteer. They slide the names of obscure cornerbacks onto magnetized walls, charting not only their selections, but those of every opponent as well.

And as soon as it's over, the scouts are arranging tryouts for two dozen undrafted free agents. Which is not to overlook NFL free agents, available for signing from mid-February through mid-July. In effect, every NFL front office becomes a corporate version of the Marrakesh bazaar. Talent is brought in, prodded gently, and assessed. Offers are made and rebuffed.

The calculations never cease. Are we too thin at defensive tackle? Can we fit the guy from Carolina under the salary cap? What if we load the back end of the deal? This time of year, the head coach rarely makes a move without consulting his offensive or defensive coordinator, his director of personnel, and his CPA.

You can see why everyone is so happy when July rolls around and the business of football gains a curious addition—an actual football.

Running back Eddie George is a workhorse—in and out of season.

NFL clubs make their training facilities available to players throughout the year.

Time trials are part of a regimented routine for prospective draft choices at the annual Scouting Combine in Indianapolis.

The Jets' Chad Pennington is one of a growing number of players who have enrolled at private training facilities during the offseason.

The NFL commands center stage each spring when it conducts its annual draft at Madison Square Garden.

Decision makers in the Cleveland Browns' war room make their draft-day selection…

...and Courtney Brown learns that he has become the first player drafted.

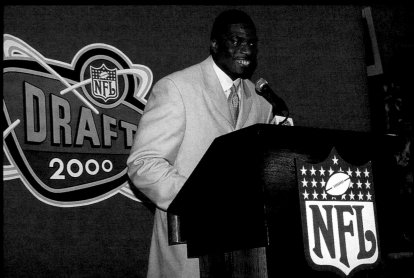

Even veteran cornerback Darrell Green extends himself at Redskins minicamp.

Daryl Gardener of the Dolphins gets his engine revved up.

Jerry Rice, the most prolific receiver in NFL history, continues working on his technique.

Brett Favre embarks on a lonely trek.

No Fun
in the
Summertime

To anyone who ever served time in an NFL training camp, the locations alone are enough to make your legs go rubbery. Wichita Falls, Texas...Stockton, California...Platteville, Wisconsin...Thibodaux, Louisiana.

They're nice places to live, but you probably wouldn't want to visit there. Not while wearing a football helmet and pads in the simmering days of July.

Training camp is the NFL without its makeup. You won't find any vivacious cheerleaders or pregame fireworks displays here. There is no danger of being blinded by stadium lights glinting off immaculately polished helmets. Nobody is miked for sound because the sound largely consists of grunts, gasps, and expletives.

"When we scout college players, we don't ask if they will play with pain," Houston Oilers coach Bum Phillips once said. "We ask 'em, do they practice with it?"

Pain—muscular, respiratory, psychological, you name it—is the main feature of training camp. This is where every football player who failed to implement a strict offseason fitness regimen gets a chance to curse himself. Those who show up in shape can curse the coaching staff.

In settings carefully selected for their combinations of heat and isolation, millionaire entertainers are treated like juvenile delinquents. They run for miles, chopped into brutal increments of 10 to 40 yards. They hit blocking sleds until they actually develop a personal dislike for the contraptions. They engage in agility drills designed to embarrass anyone large enough to play the offensive line.

Then, after what seems like 30 minutes, they do it all again. What are two-a-day practices like? Imagine backpacking five miles to a mountain retreat, then realizing you forgot your food

ERY POUND
OSE DURING
ICE, DRINK
GLASS OF
ATER

WET
FLOOR
CAUTION

The signs of training camp convey a clear message—even when misspelled.

and water purifier. You have to turn around, retrace your steps, and do it all over again.

Between practices, the players collapse in the nearest air-conditioned room, watching soap operas or SportsCenter, their minds nearly blank with exhaustion.

Besides discomfort, the primary trait of an NFL training camp is boredom. Very few camps are held in Manhattan or Miami Beach. And even if the players are resourceful enough to find ways of amusing themselves, they rarely have the energy to do so. Mostly they sit around and make small talk, trying hard not to divulge the panic that lies just under their skin. Of course, if they're feeling energetic, they can study the 150-page playbook recently compiled by the new offensive coordinator.

It isn't exactly prison because anyone is free to walk away, and the food tends to be better. The weekly shopping list from a typical Detroit Lions camp includes 200 pounds of sirloin steak, 200 pounds of prime rib, 60 pounds of bacon, 120 dozen eggs, 120 gallons of pasta sauce, 533 pieces of fruit, and, because even large men like to be treated kindly on occasion, 300 Dove Bars.

At the end of a long, hot practice session, every player knows the easiest way to cool down.

Between meals, it's pretty much a steady barrage of physical and psychological torture. The coaches don't have time to yell at everyone, so they make scapegoats of unfortunate rookie free agents, hoping the rest of the squad will absorb the lecture. More than one veteran player has learned to hold out for a renegotiated contract every other summer, with the specific intention of patching things up as training camp wanes.

The borderline players have no such luxury. Camps, scrimmages, and preseason games are their proving grounds, their stages. For most players, the hardest part of training camp is not running wind sprints or learning NFL terminology. It's the competition.

There is tremendous pressure to win during the regular season, but it can't match the bottled-up intensity of preseason, when players skirmish for starting positions and, in many cases, jobs. They come camouflaged as teammates, wearing the same colors. But this is a zero-sum game, where one man's success might mean another's professional obsolescence.

As the summer progresses, rosters that began with close to 90 names are winnowed down to 65, then 53. Slip on wet grass at the wrong time in a preseason game, or have the misfortune to play left defensive end when the opposition is concentrating on running the other direction, and you might be looking for alternative employment. Sometimes you can do everything you are asked to do and it's still not enough.

"We're letting go, often times, players who have come in and done nothing but bust their rear ends to make this team since the middle of May," Tennessee Titans head coach Jeff Fisher says. "The next morning these guys are no longer part of the program. That's a difficult thing to experience. They understand. We understand. But neither side has to like it."

The ultimate agony is that the players who come closest to making the squad—in many cases, those who worked the hardest—are cast free at the last minute, finding themselves in the poorest position to sign with another team that just set its roster.

Not that summer football is all bad. It's a time of collective optimism, when every team feels itself moving in an upward trajectory. Preseason losses are dismissed as meaningless, victories are magnified as portenders of success. Every page torn from the desk calendar is like a step toward the light. Lungs get stronger, plays get crisper.

By the end of August, the regular season rumbles like Niagara Falls, just out of sight. What is left for NFL players but to kiss the family, grip the insides of the barrel, and plunge headfirst into the spray?

Coach Steve Mariucci of the 49ers tells his players what he expects to accomplish during the day's workout.

The old-fashioned rope drill is grueling, even for a player as nimble as running back Michael Pittman.

Two-a-days are as much a mental challenge as a physical one, as offensive coordinator Sherman Lewis reminds the Vikings.

With bodies lined up nearly as far as the eye can see, practice begins with a stretching routine.

Techniques for strengthening those hard-to-reach muscles come in many forms.

Wind sprints—first, in one direction, then in the other— are a necessary evil to get in condition for the season.

Even in the Internet Age, some of the oldest training techniques are the best ones.

The Redskins quickly review
their Xs and Os.

Healthy appetites congregate in the players' dining hall, where the dress code is casual.

A whirlwind of activity surrounds Rams coach Mike Martz.

Everyone takes part in agility drills—even 276-pound John Burrough.

Ravens quarterbacks practice their footwork, performing a football ballet.

The dog days of summer are less about winning the race than they are about survival.

Training camp is an ideal place to see the stars up close—and to secure autographs from fan favorites such as Ricky Williams (below).

COUNTDOWN TO KICKOFF WEEKEND

About five minutes after the NFL releases its schedule for the upcoming season, dates get circled. Coaches, players, and fans put pens to calendars. Some guys probably even enter the data on their Palm Pilots. Anyone who is a football fan at least takes mental note, filing away the Sundays in his brain for subsequent access.

Despite the time-honored insistence that every football game is equally important, certain dates tick like time bombs. Traditional rivalries rise from the page as if carved in bas-relief. By May, every member of the Cowboys knows exactly when the Redskins invade Texas. Nationally televised prime-time games catch the eye. And if your team is scheduled to play the defending Super Bowl champion, the date seems to glow on the page. Ditto for the team that knocked you out of the playoffs last season.

So each individual calendar winds up with different marks. All different except one. Everyone circles Kickoff Weekend.

Kickoff Weekend is why NFL players scale hills in April when they could be playing 18 rounds of golf with their college roommates. It's why an offensive coordinator looks at black beans on his dinner plate and sees an exciting new offensive formation. It's why massive offensive tackles, born hungry, order from the Lite & Healthy section of the menu.

Kickoff Weekend is like a great funnel. All of the preparation of the offseason and preseason–the toil, the study, the psychological stress, the discipline, the boredom, the conquering of doubt–are stuffed into the open mouth. And out of the other end, at about a thousand miles an hour, shoots a football game.

Though separated by only a week, the regular-season opener bears only remote resemblance to the final preseason game. A first-time observer would have a hard time pinpointing the change. The players look the same. The passes travel in the

The roar of the crowd and the sense of anticipation signal the start of a new season.

same spirals, the bodies still crash together in highway pileups.

But notice the differences. Intensity virtually crackles between the goal lines. You can't see the players' faces from your seats in section 215, but you know their eyes are bulging and their jaws are clenched. The game plans have evolved, too. Gone is the steady diet of off-tackle runs and standard defenses, replaced by play-action passing and sadistic blitz schemes. Just as important to the overall effect, the sporadic fan involvement of the preseason has evolved into frenzied tribal war chants.

Both teams are absolutely certain they're going to win this football game. They radiate confidence. Their preparations have advanced with the building excitement of a Broadway opening. Everything started clumsy and disorganized. The stars kept bumping into one another. But as the summer progressed, the choreography got tighter and the players more confident. By the time September rolls around, 100 dissonant voices have become a chorus.

Thirty-one teams, and every one of them uttering the same certainty: "We can win this year."

"It's like a birthday," says Junior Seau, San Diego's fiery linebacker. "It's the birth of a new year and a new era. And you never know what's going to happen. There's so much curiosity about what a team has been hiding in the preseason. There's your birthday surprise. Hopefully, you can open it with a smile."

Sometimes the box is empty. Sometimes you don't like the surprise. With better luck, you can be like the St. Louis Rams of 1999. The most downtrodden franchise of the previous decade, starting an obscure quarterback, opened the season with a 27-10 victory over Baltimore. A lot of people laughed it off and waited for the pratfall. But this time the victory was exactly what it appeared to be, the signal of a monumental turnaround.

And that's the beauty of Kickoff Weekend. Half the teams that play on Kickoff Weekend will win their first game in 2001, and every one of them will herald the triumph as proof of its imminent rise. Half the teams will lose and shrug it off as one small setback in a 16-game season.

Meanwhile, fans can relish the excitement of an NFL Sunday. For months they bided time, waiting for this moment. They made honorable attempts to watch baseball, even as they struggled to remember what inning it was. They replaced windows and went fishing, but in the backs of their minds small voices kept whispering, "Check the list of NFL free-agent signings."

Unfurled banners greet the Buccaneers at their home opener.

Fans have high aspirations of their own. But to most of them, victory isn't as important as the experience itself. Kickoff Weekend is part of the ritual of their lives, a notch marking time's progress, as intrinsic to the fall as leaves turning colors.

People talk about the "comforts" of autumn. To many of us, this has little to do with sweaters and sweet potatoes and a chill in the air. To a real football fan, true comfort consists of a remote control and a capacity crowd in the living room, Vikings-Packers on one channel and Dolphins-Jets on another.

Clenched jaws and piercing eyes reflect the Rams' intensity before their home opener.

An explosion of colors heralds the start of the Pittsburgh Steelers' season...

...and a military flyover sets the stage for the Baltimore Ravens' kickoff.

Understated discipline defines the Buffalo Bills' arrival on the field...

...while Prime Time flamboyance is part of Deion Sanders's introduction in Washington.

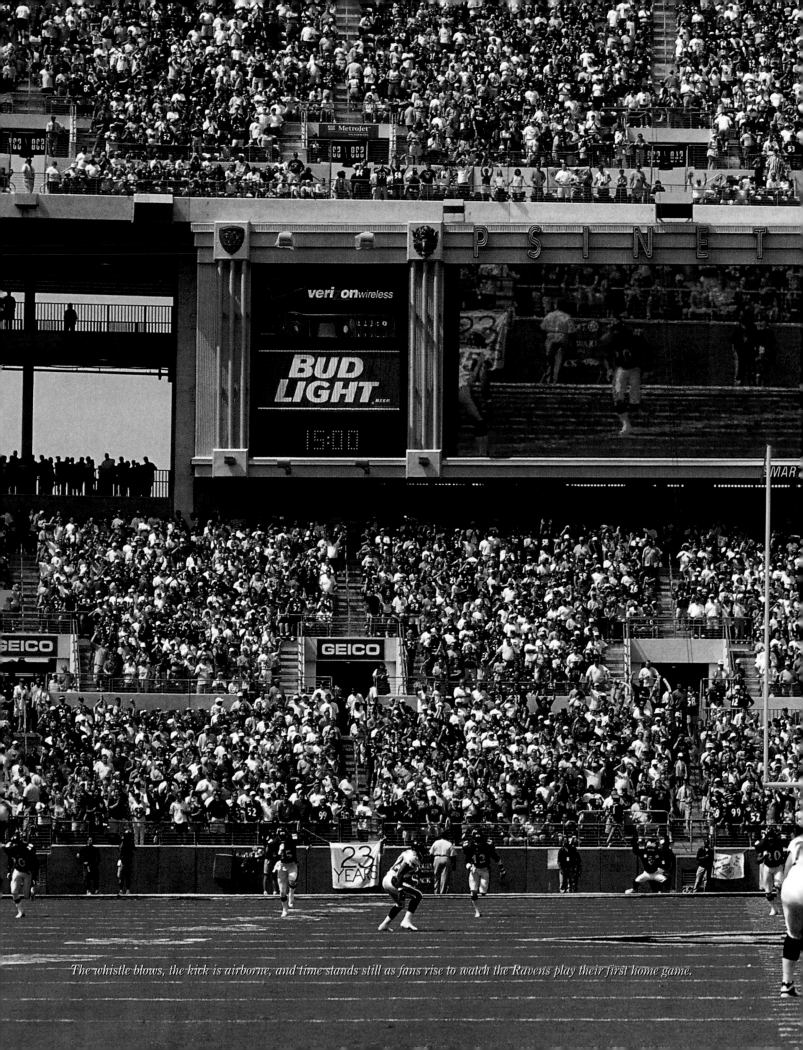

The whistle blows, the kick is airborne, and time stands still as fans rise to watch the Ravens play their first home game.

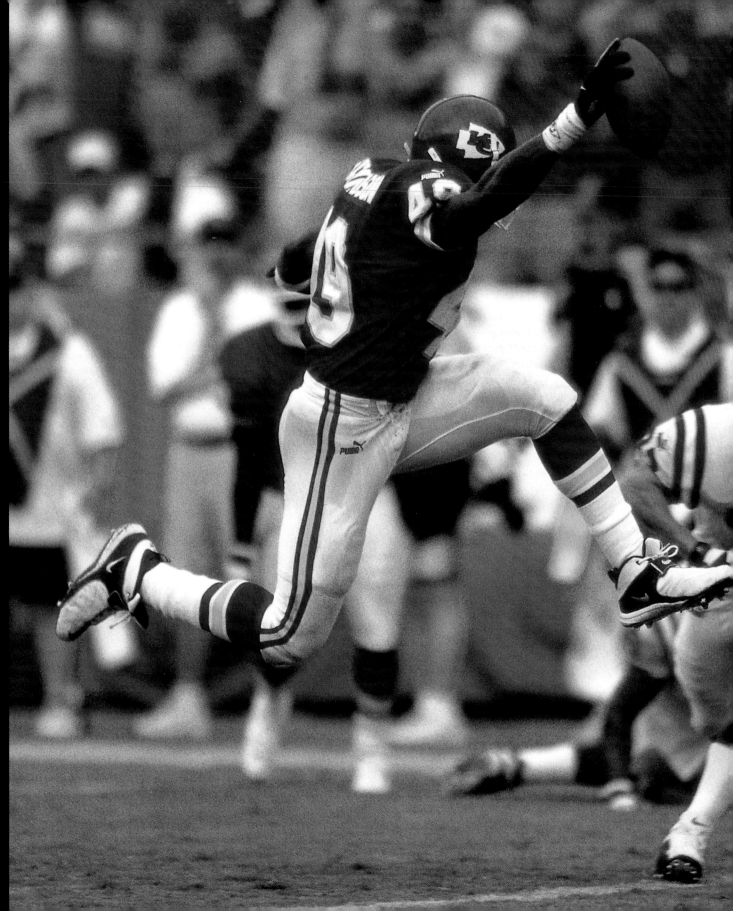

Redskins defensive end Marco Coleman welcomes Carolina quarterback Steve Beuerlein to the 2000 season.

Tony Richardson exults, but only briefly. The Colts defeated the Chiefs 27-14.

The hitting is harder in the regular season, as Eric Warfield reminds the Colts' Edgerrin James.

Fullback Fred Beasley hits paydirt against the Falcons—1 of 3 touchdowns he scored in the game.

On a day of lofty expectations, the Vikings' Daunte Culpepper goes airborne against the Bears.

Plaxico Burress and Duane Starks engage in hand-to-hand combat.

When the season kicks off, 13-year veteran Tim Brown shifts into high gear for the Raiders.

After the long-awaited first game: physically exhausted and emotionally drained.

FACES OF GAME DAY TELL THEIR OWN STORY

It is noon on an October Sunday, and the football people are scurrying like worker ants. It might be ALLTEL Stadium, or 3Com Park, or Adelphia Coliseum. The team colors change, the bustle does not.

The parking-lot attendants are smiling broadly and accepting $10 bills. Teenagers with electric torches are herding minivans as if they're taxiing DC-10s. In the shadow of the stadium, the staff dispenses tickets, each one as magical as the gold note in a Willy Wonka bar. Fifty paces away, the gate attendants unceremoniously rip them in half.

The modern-day NFL stadium is a thriving, self-contained city for at least 10 dates each year. Cops, paramedics, tow-truck drivers, waiters, and bartenders all remain on duty, hoping the disturbances are minor and the tips large. An army of vendors sells everything from *NFL Insider* programs to jalapeño-sprinkled nachos to satin jackets. Above the stadium, blimps and biplanes circle like carousel horses.

The activity quickens as the clock advances. The event staff scowls, the ushers wink, the National Anthem singer clears her throat. The tuba player throws a wadded-up napkin at a woodwind.

Halfway up the rows of seats, a Plexiglas-ensconced succession of suites and booths sparkles like a vein of quartz. There the mood is quietly nervous. The radio and TV guys make their pregame reports as the public-address announcer mentions the upcoming visit by the Colts. That pricks up the ears of Indianapolis's advance scout, who is preparing play charts in the press box. He's hiding among several dozen reporters, most of whom are finding fault with the hometown quarterback and/or eating free hot dogs. Next door to them, the replay official and his assistant are checking their equipment. One more booth down the line, a technician in the scoreboard control room has to smile

The NFL shield goes up long before the first fans arrive at Cleveland Browns Stadium.

as he posts: "AMY, WILL YOU MARRY ME? LOVE, SEAN."

On the field, the photographers are dressed for battle, armed with high-speed shutters and staking out positions. The grounds crew searches for divots or uneven seams. And while the head trainers and equipment men ply their trades in the locker room, their helpers busily arrange tidy rows of footballs, bandages, and Gatorade cups next to the benches. The cheerleaders are catching the eyes of male spectators and inciting marital spats. The chain gang and spotters stand at attention, dressed in black-and-white and fully prepared to order the world in 10-yard increments.

It's a complex and immense division of labor, the world's biggest circus. And let's not forget the trained Bears, snarling Lions, soaring Eagles, and other active participants.

A "must-win" game is a redundancy in the NFL, where you get only 16 chances to live past December. One game can dump you out of the playoffs, one play can win or lose a game, and the precise positioning of your right shoulder can make or break you on a given play. This precariousness is not lost on the players or coaches. It follows that the atmosphere preceding an NFL game tends to be slightly more intense than the moments after a National Weather Service tornado warning.

The common image of an NFL dressing room has players roaring and banging their heads against lockers. In reality, this is true only of linebackers and fullbacks. Most of their teammates are too busy studying playbooks, computer printouts, Polaroid snapshots, and Bible verses. Some listen to their Walkmans…the final calm before the storm.

The coaching staff has had more than four days to analyze the opponent and prepare its troops, but it's never enough. So the head coach fine tunes his game plan at the last minute, the changes trickling down through the ranks.

Meanwhile, in another locker room, the officiating crew

Sunday is a busy day for an NFL ticket taker.

rehashes recent edicts, controversies, and interpretations of the intentional-grounding rule. These seven men know they will be all but invisible for the next three hours, except on those few occasions when the entire populace wants to pummel them.

Why do they do it? Why do the writers write and the cheerleaders cheer? Why do the coaches study Red Zone tendencies until they have bags under their eyes? Why do players run on taped-over sprained ankles and pretend they don't hurt? There are many reasons. The easy answer is that they're compensated to do so.

And the reason they're paid participants in a weekly diversion is that for millions of Americans, NFL Sunday is what gets them through the rest of the week. The cameras, the scoreboards, the press box—they're like the skeletal system of NFL football. What animates the game is the fans.

Not that you can pigeonhole these people. The United States isn't necessarily the melting pot it claims to be, but it comes close on NFL Sunday. In sports bars from Bangor, Maine, to Escondido, California, lawyers and roofers and fixed-income retirees rub elbows and exchange high-fives. They often have little in common, except for their unbridled love of the Bills or the Chiefs or the Cowboys and an equally powerful disdain for this week's opponents.

On game day, the parking lot of an NFL stadium is like a town picnic. People fold tacos and stir gumbo side by side, discussing the two-minute offense. A Nerf football is in the air, and everyone in parking zone J8 is an eligible receiver.

Here there are no computer glitches. There are no overdue rents or barking dogs. This is a place of pure emotional release and ritualized comfort. It's not a lot different than it was in 1965. The jersey might say FAVRE instead of STARR, but the bratwurst smells the same and the game is compelling.

This is NFL football, and it keeps us coming back.

Real fans—the kind who show up early—have no compunction about displaying their allegiance.

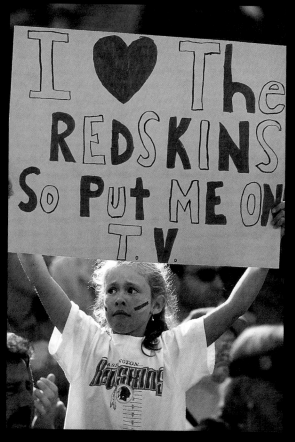

A team's biggest supporter sometimes comes in the smallest package.

The atmosphere surrounding game day is like a town picnic, as neighbors and friends become kindred spirits.

The Carolina Panthers are the best team in the league.

...unless, of course, you happen to be a Miami Dolphins' fan.

A grounds crew relies on football-like teamwork to replace a damaged section of artificial turf.

*Another day at the office
for broadcasters John
Madden and Pat
Summerall*

In the moments before kickoff:

a patriotic ritual

Dolphins Cheerleaders rev up the crowd in Miami.

Old, young, male, and female: All hail the Packers!

A Redskins' game is regarded as a religious experience in the nation's capital.

In the heart of true Vikings fa see purple.

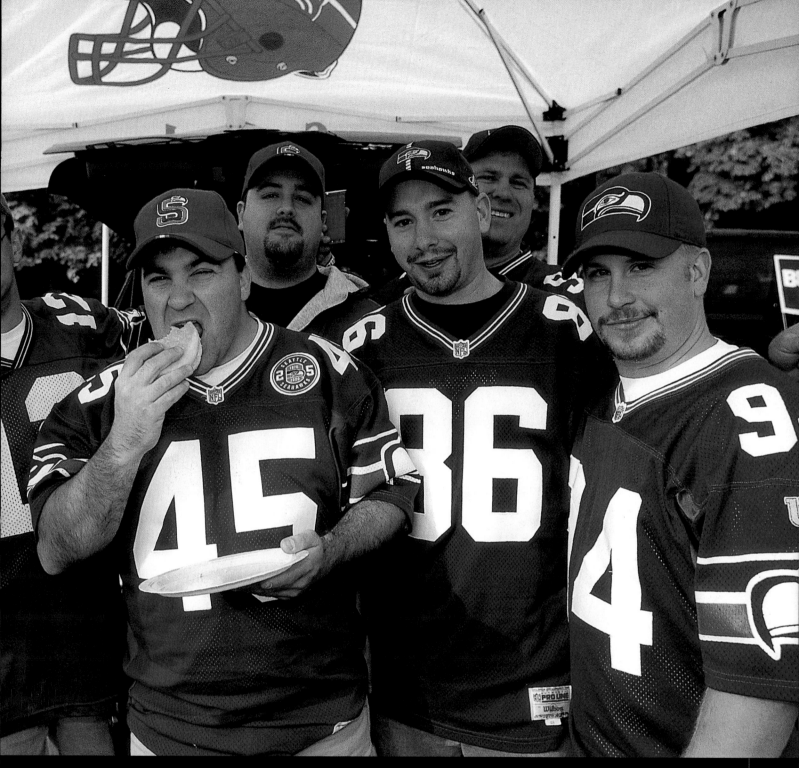

These Seahawks fans feast on a Sunday afternoon of football.

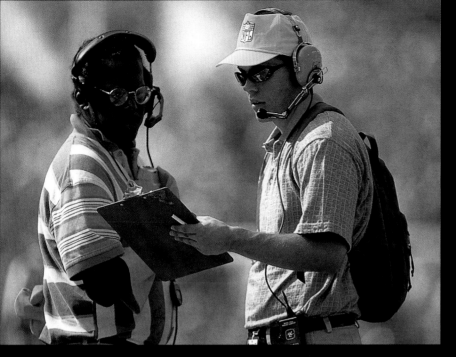

An NFL game is the product of many parts. Clockwise from top left: A sideline official (green hat) coordinates game interruptions and TV time outs; a ballboy stands at the ready; security personnel huddle before kickoff; an official positions sideline yard markers.

Overlooked but indispensable: the chain gang (left)

*Because every NFL game is televised, cameramen
are a familiar sight on game day. The ears (left)
and eyes (above) of the telecast bring the game into
millions of homes across the nation.*

A SEASON OF UPS AND DOWNS

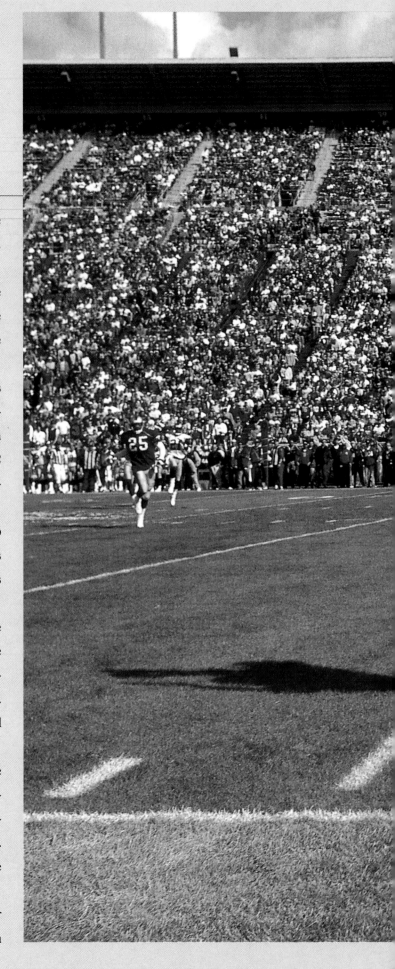

Week 1: Your favorite team rolls to victory at home in the season opener, outgaining its opponent by 155 yards. Monday's headline in the sports page: "Super Bowl Bound?"

Week 2: Your team disintegrates in its first road game amidst a flurry of penalties, turnovers, and sacks. Callers to the local radio sports-talk show speculate that the victory in the first game was an aberration.

Week 3: When the young starting quarterback struggles through 2½ quarters, the coach benches him. The veteran back-up then leads the team on two sustained drives in the fourth quarter and throws a game-winning touchdown pass with 42 seconds left. The city immediately divides into warring quarterback camps.

Week 4: The offense clicks on all cylinders, setting club records for first downs and rushing yardage. Yet the game goes down to the wire, courtesy of a porous defense. The linebackers appear to be tackling with arms made of soggy kelp.

Week 5: After a players-only meeting that necessitates the replacement of several pieces of office furniture, the defense stiffens. A more aggressive blitz scheme nets 5 sacks, 4 knock-downs, 9 hurries, and 1 harried opposing quarterback. Curiously, the offense picks the same week to take a nap, and the game again goes down to the wire.

Week 6: For the first time in weeks, the offense and the defense simultaneously play up to capabilities. Your team controls the line of scrimmage and grinds out a 13-minute advantage in time of possession, but the special teams break down. One punt is blocked, another returned for a touchdown. The rookie from Fresno State fumbles 2 kickoffs in a 24-20 loss.

Week 7: A bye week. Fans bite their fingernails and pace for most of two weeks, while coaches pile on homework like a

The Rams' Jacoby Shepherd (22) and the 49ers' Tai Streets wage a lonely battle amid 68,000 onlookers at 3Com Park.

sadistic ninth-grade civics teacher. At least one member of the team is quoted as saying, "The bye couldn't have come at a better time for us."

Week 8: The left inside linebacker vaults over a pile of writhing bodies, stopping a runner at the goal line to preserve a victory. The hero had been listed as questionable prior to the game, but was able to play thanks to the equipment manager, who rigged up a special neck brace to protect the player's pinched nerve. The brace resembles a medieval torture device.

Week 9: One of the most exciting games of the season is a loss. Scoring plays include a 58-yard fumble return by a pear-shaped defensive tackle, a 75-yard pass that ricochets off a cornerback's facemask, and a naked bootleg that the quarterback finishes with a clumsy dive to the left pylon. Meanwhile, the right tackle and left defensive end exchange more than words. They hammer, punch, and curse one another from the opening kickoff to the final gun, each dropping in exhaustion at the end.

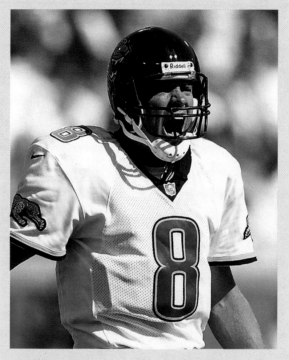

Mark Brunell barks orders to the Jaguars.

Week 10: A promising season turns precarious when the star halfback sprains a ligament in his left knee. His backup has good speed and instincts, but little experience. The kid's move into the starting lineup means coaches have to scramble to fill positions on special teams. With determination, incredibly expensive rehab equipment, and the doting attention of the team's trainers, the star will be back in a month.

Week 11: The head coach is a vehement opponent of instant replay as an officiating aid. This time, he challenges a key third-down reception in the fourth quarter, and the referee rules in his favor. Upon further review, the coach says, "This system is good for the game."

Week 12: The backup runner breaks loose for 137 yards,

making geniuses of the team's scouting department. The back publicly thanks his offensive line after the game. Privately, he thinks of his grandfather, who called on Saturday to say, "You keep your head up, boy. You deserve this chance. And no matter what happens tomorrow, I'm damn proud of you."

Week 13: The kicker nails a 49-yard field goal as time expires and rides his teammates' arms like the lead singer in a mosh pit. Everyone in earshot expresses their affection for the little guy and affirms his importance to the team.

Week 14: The same kicker misses an extra point and 3 field goals, including a potential game winner with 1:12 left. He is a locker-room pariah. No one speaks to him, looks at him, or otherwise acknowledges his existence.

Week 15: The offensive coordinator, who calls the team's plays, is mobbed by reporters after his quarterback directs a 74-yard scoring drive in the final minutes. They want to know what the coach had seen to make him believe he could exploit the left side of the opponent's secondary. The coordinator sheepishly admits that the quarterback's helmet radio receiver was kaput throughout the drive and that all plays were called on the field.

Week 16: All season long, a rookie safety has been burned in the same pass-coverage rotation. No matter how many times he practiced the scheme, he failed to master it—until now. Undermining the opponent's film work, he comes up with 2 big interceptions. "I"d expect nothing less from the guy," the coach says. "He's not a rookie anymore."

Week 17: The team wins at home in its final game, grabbing the last wild-card spot in the conference. Monday's headline in the local sports page: "Super Bowl Bound?"

This is the roller coaster that is the NFL regular season.

Linebacker John Mobley reacts after the Broncos stand firm on defense.

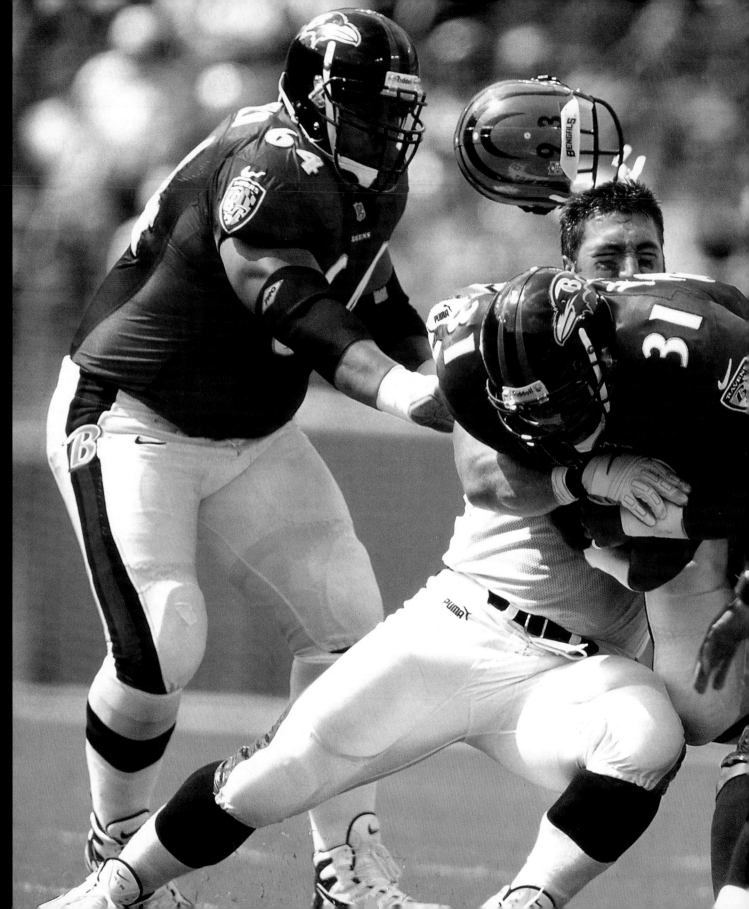

The Patriots cut off quarterback Peyton Manning at the pass.

The Ravens' Jamal Lewis (31) meets Tom Barndt of the Bengals in a head-turning collision.

Brian Griese tries to gather himself on a frustrating day...

...and Trace Armstrong celebrates after a big play.

*With Chiefs cornerback Eric Warfield hot on his trail, the
Titans' Carl Pickens goes airborne in the end zone.*

Wayne Chrebet of the Jets searches for the handle on a misfired pass.

Derrick Mayes of the Seahawks eyeballs a fingertip reception against the Jaguars.

Keyshawn Johnson zeroes in on a catch, despite the defensive efforts of Minnesota's Robert Tate.

Bill Schroeder finds a pot of gold at the end of a rainbow pass from Brett Favre.

*A silver-and-black celebration greets the
Raiders' Tyrone Wheatley...*

...and Minnesota's Randy Moss inspires purple pride.

Arizona's MarTay Jenkins abruptly comes to a stop as David Terrell stakes a claim to his leg.

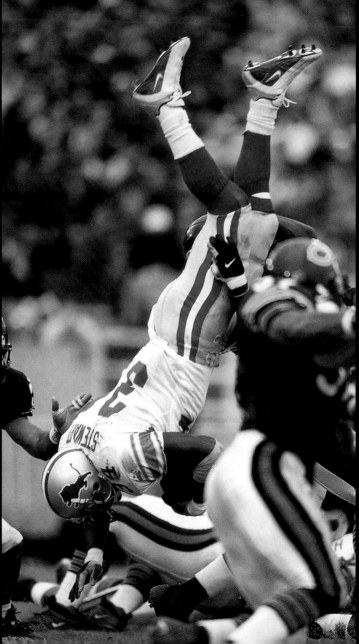

James Stewart of the Lions goes heels over head.

At the end of a long day, Jim Harbaugh (above) deals with defeat...and friendly foes Aeneas Williams and Donovan McNabb (right) acknowledge a game well played.

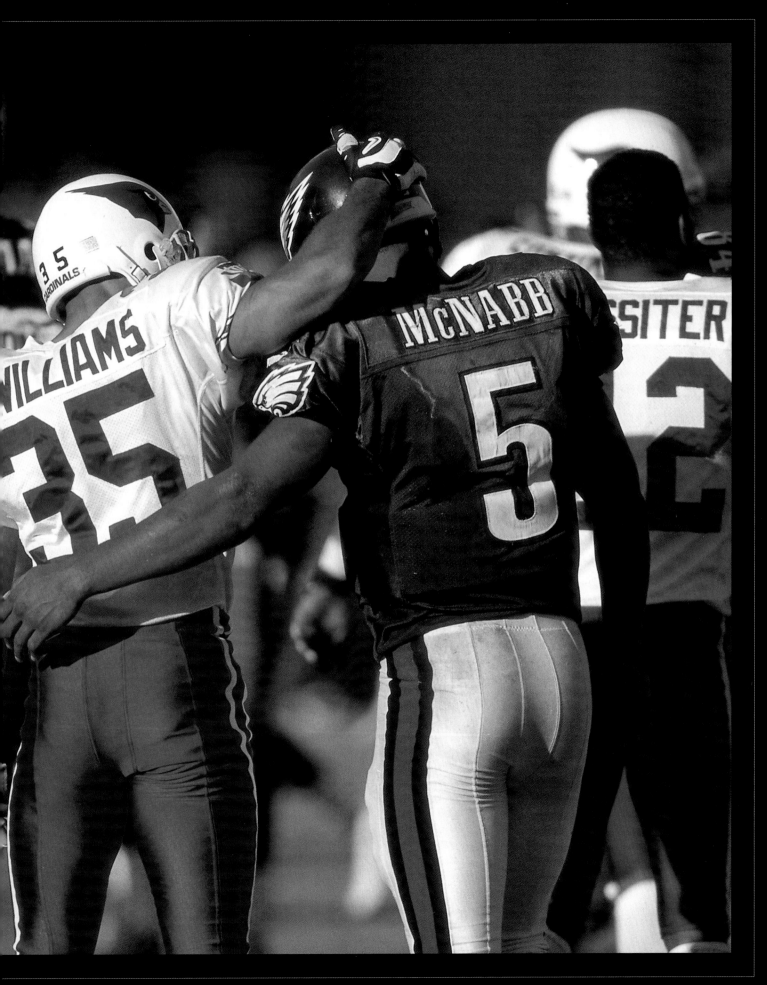

THE ROAD
TO THE
SUPER BOWL

Early January is when you start to wonder whether the NFL isn't just a brilliantly conceived video game.

Okay, so we've ridden through fire on a unicycle, withstood a full frontal assault from Kublai Khan's horsemen, and blasted a squadron of aliens who shoot exploding pellets from their noses. And our reward for such heroics? A gold crown? A free game? No, it's a ticket to the next level, where we encounter a crazed Minotaur with a bazooka.

The NFL season is only slightly less absurd. Think about it. Teams face one determined opponent after another, with only the slightest chance to catch their breath in between. The action comes in waves, like the surf pounding against a breakwater. NFL teams work through injuries—some debilitating, some merely painful. They overcome doubts, mechanical flaws, and personality conflicts. If they survive a grueling 16-game season and earn a playoff berth, their reward is to start over again.

When Marv Levy coached the Bills, he spoke of the "extra season" they weathered, referring to the 13 postseason games they played from 1990-93. Levy wasn't complaining, nor does anyone else who earns the chance for playoff duty. That's because the only thing worse than competing in the postseason is *not* competing in the postseason.

"I used to tell people I would play for free, I would practice for free," says retired linebacker Clay Matthews, "but they had to pay me to sit through those meetings day after day. But you do it all—all of the sprints, all of the work in the offseason, something every day to get ready—because you want a chance at the whole thing. And you kind of say to yourself, 'Please just let me play for it all. That's all I want.'"

Matthews labored for 19 seasons (1978-1996) and was voted to the Pro Bowl four times. And guess what? He never

Donovan McNabb eludes Tampa Bay's Tyoka Jackson during the Eagles' 21-3 victory in an NFC Wild Card Game.

played for it all. He never got to the Super Bowl. On the bright side, he did get to the playoffs. That's more than legendary Bears players Dick Butkus and Gale Sayers can claim.

Athletes rising from the college ranks to the NFL often speak of how the game "speeds up" at the pro level. Running backs hit the holes sooner; receivers gain separation for an instant, then are blanketed again; passes arrive so fast that sometimes they are caught in self-defense. Amazingly, the action has yet another speed: playoff speed.

"That guy on the other side of the ball is trying to take my money or take my ring," Raiders fullback Zack Crockett said. "You have all that playing in your mind, and it's faster out there."

It's more intense out there, and that has to do with a lot more than postseason revenue shares.

There are no seven-game series in the NFL playoffs, as other sports leagues employ. There is no time to regroup, to lick your wounds, and juggle the lineup. This is the gladiator ring, the essence of "do or die." If you are victorious in the NFL playoffs, you stay alive for one more week and get ready for the next challenge. If you lose, you pack your bags and start reliving those two or three botched plays that will haunt you for the next several months.

Considering the inherent desperation built into the NFL postseason—the precarious, giddy tension that separates glory

Lamar Smith sets sail on 1 of his 40 carries against the Colts, on a day when he gained 209 rushing yards.

and failure—it makes sense that the playoffs have produced some of the gridiron's most memorable moments. The biggest blowout in league history came in the postseason (73-0, Bears over the Redskins in the 1940 NFL Championship Game), as did the greatest comeback (32 points, Levy's Bills over the Oilers in a 1992 AFC Wild Card Game).

Only in a playoff atmosphere, with an impending loss hanging over Three Rivers Stadium like a storm cloud, could a rookie named Franco Harris pluck a deflected ball off his shoe tops—deflected by whom, we may never know—and race down the sideline like a ghost, almost single-handedly altering the fate of recession-era Pittsburgh with his Immaculate Reception. Only in the fishbowl of the postseason could Minnesota's Gary Anderson miss a 38-yard field goal after making 123 consecutive kicks, leaving the door ajar for the resilient Falcons to win the 1998 NFC Championship Game.

The Ice Bowl, the Hail Mary, Ghost to the Post, the Catch, the Drive, and the Music City Miracle. They are moments that linger in our memories. These games are products of great athleticism and bravery, borne of the NFL's postseason structure, which engenders fear, hope, and anxiety in equal portions.

As fans, we hardly can bring ourselves to watch these games. Once we do, we scarcely can look away.

After latching on to a deflected pass, Shannon Sharpe sheds a Broncos' defender and eyes the goal line.

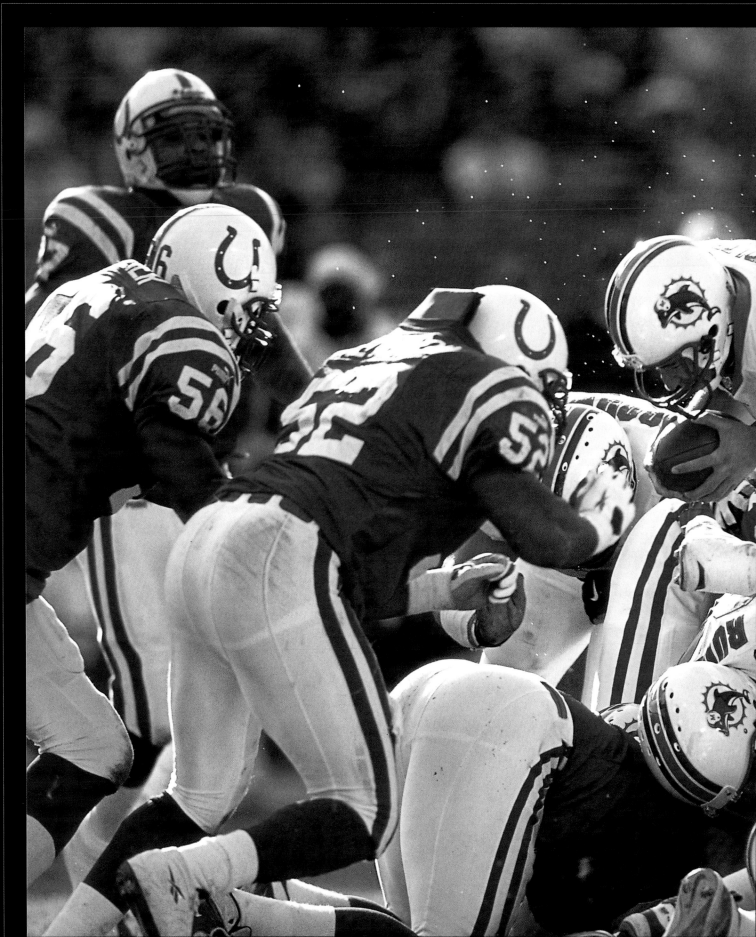

Miami's Jay Fiedler goes airborne—and braces for a collision.

Running back Jamal Lewis of the Ravens is on top of the world, if only briefly.

Cris Carter snares a 17-yard touchdown pass beyond the outstretched arm of the Saints' Kevin Mathis.

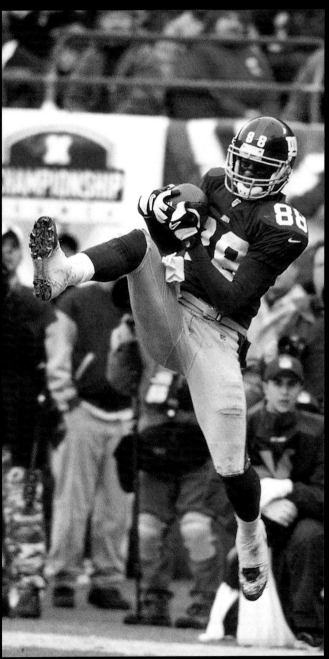

Ike Hilliard makes an acrobatic touchdown reception to help the Giants win the NFC title.

The Ravens' relentless defense buries Eddie George in a divisional playoff game...

...and grounds the Raiders' Rich Gannon in the AFC Championship Game.

The Rams' Kurt Warner feels the wrath of an inspired Saints' defense.

Daunte Culpepper receives an unexpected visit from the Giants' Michael Strahan.

After an impromptu Gatorade bath...

...coach Jim Fassel and the Super Bowl-bound Giants
enjoy the spoils of victory.

Confetti rains on the AFC champion Baltimore Ravens.

ON TOP OF
THE FOOTBALL
WORLD

To gauge the meaning of a Super Bowl victory—to understand the depth of sport's most publicized accomplishment—begin by considering the story of Lyle Alzado.

Alzado, who died of cancer in 1992, was a defensive end from 1971-1985. He was the NFL's ultimate tough guy, a bareknuckled brawler from Brooklyn. Alzado played each game as if the man across the line owed him money. It was Alzado, don't forget, who once said, "If me and King Kong went into an alley, only one of us would come out. And it wouldn't be the monkey."

By January, 1984, Alzado had logged 13 NFL seasons and had yet to win a Super Bowl ring. He played for Denver in Super Bowl XII, but the Broncos were crushed by Dallas. Alzado moved on to Cleveland, then to the Los Angeles Raiders. Super Bowl XVIII was his last realistic shot at a championship, and as the lopsided game wound down in the fourth quarter, it was clear the Raiders would win.

When the television cameras found Alzado on the sideline, he was neither pounding his chest nor baring his teeth. He was not dancing or hugging or praying. He stood there near the Raiders' bench, fidgeting and watching the seconds tick away on the Tampa Stadium game clock. All of the trials and setbacks of a 13-year career were in his eyes. Bloodshot and blinking, they were tiny lakes—watery reservoirs contained not by steel and concrete, but by the sheer will of an NFL tough guy who was determined not to blubber on national television.

Few of us have been in Alzado's position, so it's hard to imagine how he felt that evening. Sports are unique in that we can point to the best, with some objective certainty, in any given year. We can't be sure about the world's greatest mortgage broker or the most talented dry cleaner in the country. We can't even agree on the year's best motion picture.

RAYMOND JAMES STADIUM

HESS

000

The eyes of the sports world focus on the Baltimore Ravens in the moments after Super Bowl XXXV.

The Super Bowl eliminates such quandaries in the world of football. It puts two teams in an alley, and only one of them walks out. The outcome immediately absorbs the weight of historical significance, the winner's name etched forever onto the sterling silver Vince Lombardi Trophy. Self-worth? A Super Bowl victory brings immortality.

That's why NFL players will do almost anything to get one. It's why the Rams' Jack Youngblood played all of Super Bowl XIV on a broken leg, and why the Steelers' Dwight White ignored the effects of pleurisy, climbing out of a hospital bed to face the Vikings in Super Bowl IX.

The pursuit of immortality is why Doug Williams, the first African-American quarterback to play in the Super Bowl, never considered retiring to the Washington sidelines after painfully hyperextending his knee late in the first quarter of game XXII. "At that point, tomorrow didn't matter," Williams says. "If I never got a chance to play another game of football again, it wouldn't have mattered. You know, you want to get paid, you want to be secure financially, but the epitome of playing professional football is to play and win the Super Bowl. And I made it that far."

Then there is the other side: losing the Super Bowl.

Marv Levy's Buffalo Bills are sometimes ridiculed as the failures of the 1990s. Their crime? Winning four consecutive AFC championships, then losing four subsequent games to strong NFC foes. The Bills came within one play of beating the Giants in Super Bowl XXV. But a game-ending field-goal attempt that drifted agonizingly wide of its target denied them the Lombardi Trophy.

Dallas defensive tackle Bob Lilly was so outraged at losing Super Bowl V, he threw his helmet 50 yards after the game—

An unmistakable visitor glides above Raymond James Stadium during the pregame ceremony.

and didn't even remember doing it. The Colts' pain at being upset by the Jets in Super Bowl III was so great that owner (and New York resident) Carroll Rosenbloom never got over it. He and coach Don Shula parted company a year after the loss.

"I felt like one of the losers at Pompeii," Chiefs running back Curtis McClinton said of falling to Green Bay in the first clash of AFL and NFL champions. "I was overwhelmed by the feeling that there would never be another Super Bowl game or another football season. It was like being on a deathbed."

Redskins coach George Allen disagreed only by degree. "Losing the Super Bowl is worse than death," he said, reflecting on a defeat at the hands of Shula's Dolphins in VII. "You have to get up the next morning."

With stakes this high, it's no wonder that even a coach as venerable as Lombardi, whose name is synonymous with football's ultimate game, was "shaking like a leaf" before his Packers took the field for the first Super Bowl. It's not surprising that even Joe Montana, the quarterback who defined big-game cool, nearly hyperventilated in XXIII while directing the most famous drive in Super Bowl history.

That perspective helps us understand why 200,000 people would brave a frigid rain, lining up along Pratt Street and Gay Street and in Baltimore's War Memorial Plaza, to greet the victorious Ravens last January.

"We came so close time and time again, but no cigar," longtime NFL owner Art Modell said after his Ravens had defeated the Giants in Super Bowl XXXV. "Now comes the cigar."

A lot of good men waited a long time to savor that cigar, guys such as Jim Plunkett, Walter Payton, and John Elway. Each discovered what Modell now knows: Nothing in all of sports tastes sweeter.

Defensive end Michael McCrary separates Giants quarterback Kerry Collins from the football.

Quarterback Trent Dilfer's voice hangs in the air in the seconds before the Ravens and Giants collide at midfield.

Trent Dilfer (above) expresses his sentiments after the Ravens' Brandon Stokley (80) slipped past Jason Sehorn for a 38-yard touchdown reception.

Despite watching the giant video screen to see Dave Thomas lunge for him,
Qadry Ismail cannot avoid being tackled on this 44-yard gain.

Ravens cornerback Chris McAlister intercepts a pass to foil a Giants' scoring threat just before halftime.

For the first time in Super Bowl history, kickoffs are returned for touchdowns on back-to-back plays—first, by the Giants' Ron Dixon (below), and then by the Ravens' Jermaine Lewis.

Jamal Lewis dives for the end zone and the Ravens' final touchdown in a 34-7 victory.

Linebacker Ray Lewis, the Super Bowl MVP, readies himself for the next snap.

Ravens coach Brian Billick (left) embraces Art Modell, the venerable club owner who finally won a Super Bowl.

PHOTOGRAPHY CREDITS

(Legend: T=top, B=bottom, L=left, R=right)

Page 1: David Stluka; **2-3**: Garrett Ellwood; **5**: Allen Kee; **6-7**: Michael Burr; **8**: NFLP/Paul Spinelli; **9**: Michael Burr;

10-11: Michael Zagaris; **12-13**: Al Messerschmidt; **13R**: Andy Hayt; **14-15**: NFLP/Kevin Terrell; **16-17**: Jimmy Cribb;

18-19: Al Messerschmidt; **20L**: Ron Vesely; **20-21**: NFLP/Paul Spinelli; **22-23**: Al Messerschmidt; **23R**: Al Messerschmidt;

24-25: Baron Wolman; **26-27**: NFLP/Kevin Terrell; **28-29**: Bill Stover; **30**: NFLP/Rob Brown; **31**: Joe Patronite;

32-33: Joe Patronite; **34L**: NFLP/Kevin Terrell; **34-35**: Al Messerschmidt; **36-37**: Al Messerschmidt; **38-39**: John Reid;

39R: Al Messerschmidt; **40**: Scott Cunningham; **41**: Al Messerschmidt; **42-43**: James Biever; **43R**: Michael Zagaris;

44-45: Michael Zagaris; **46**: Michael Zagaris; **47**: Michael Zagaris; **48-49**: Mike Allen; **49R**: Mike Moore; **50-51**: Bill Stover;

52-53: Miguel Elliot; **52B**: Greg Crisp; **53R**: Al Messerschmidt; **54L**: Bill Wood; **54-55**: Michael Zagaris; **56**: Bill Stover;

57: Mike Allen; **58-59**: Al Messerschmidt; **60**: Mike Fabus; **61T**: Peter Read Miller; **61B**: Michael Hebert;

62-63: G. Newman Lowrance; **64**: Al Messerschmidt; **65**: Rick Yeatts; **66**: NFLP/Paul Spinelli; **67**: Greg Crisp;

68L: David Drapkin; **68-69**: Garrett Ellwood; **70-71**: Cappy Jackson; **72-73**: G. Newman Lowrance; **73R**: Marty Morrow;

74: Joe Robbins; **75**: Michael Zagaris; **76-77**: Mark Brettingen; **78**: Mike Fabus; **79**: Greg Trott; **80-81**: Bill Wood;

82-83: Joe Patronite; **84**: NFLP/Greg Trott; **85**: Al Messerschmidt; **86L**: NFLP/Paul Spinelli; **86-87**: Al Messerschmidt;

88: Al Pereira; **89**: Steven Murphy; **90-91**: Al Pereira; **91R**: NFLP/Kevin Terrell; **92L**: Al Messerschmidt;

92-93: Steven Murphy; **94-95**: David Stluka; **96T**: Al Messerschmidt; **96B**: Al Messerschmidt; **97**: NFLP/Joe Patronite;

98: NFLP/James Smith; **99TL**: John Reid; **99BL**: Greg Trott; **99TR**: David Drapkin; **99BR**: Al Messerschmidt;

100L: James Smith; **100-101**: James Smith; **102-103**: Bernie Nuñez; **104**: Al Messerschmidt; **105**: Joe Patronite;

106-107: Bernie Nuñez; **107R**: Tony Tomsic; **108**: Joe Poellot; **109**: Al Messerschmidt; **110-111**: Allen Kee;

112: Henry Ordosgoitia; **113**: Al Messerschmidt; **114**: Joe Robbins; **115**: G. Newman Lowrance; **116**: Greg Trott;

117: Mark Brettingen; **118-119**: Allen Kee; **119R**: David Drapkin; **120L**: NFLP/Kevin Terrell; **120-121**: Greg Trott;

122-123: Greg Crisp; **124**: Paul Jasienski; **125**: Bill Wood; **126-127**: Allen Kee; **128**: Bill Wood; **129**: Joe Robbins;

130-131: Vincent Muzik; **131R**: Greg Crisp; **132**: Joe Patronite; **133**: Peter Brouillet; **134-135**: Joe Patronite;

135R: Allen Kee; **136L**: Joe Robbins; **136-137**: John Reid; **138-139**: Mike Moore; **140-141**: NFLP/Kevin Terrell;

142: Michael Zagaris; **143**: Richard Mackson; **144-145**: NFLP/Kevin Terrell; **146-147**: Al Messerschmidt;

147R: Evan Pinkus; **148-149**: David Drapkin; **150-151**: NFLP/Kevin Terrell; **152L**: Al Messerschmidt;

152-153: Jimmy Cribb; **154**: Michael Zagaris; **155**: David Drapkin; **156-157**: Allen Kee; **158**: Richard Mackson.